First published in Great Britain in 2006 and in the USA in 2007 by
Frances Lincoln Children's Books, 4 Torriano Mews, Torriano Avenue, London NW5 2RZ

www.franceslincoln.com

Distributed in the USA by Publishers Group West

British Library Cataloguing in Publication Data available on request

ISBN 10: 1-84507-295-2
ISBN 13: 978-1-84507-295-7

Printed in China

1 3 5 7 9 8 6 4 2

Young Gardener

Stefan & Beverley Buczacki

Special photography by Anthea Sieveking

FRANCES LINCOLN
CHILDREN'S BOOKS

Contents

Dear Young Gardener

We have written this book because we love gardening and our garden.
We began gardening when we were young, helping our parents, and
although there were times when we were too busy to do much gardening,
our love of growing things never left us. We hope it will be the same
for you too.

Gardening is something you do because you enjoy it. We don't expect
you to garden all the time, but try to set aside a small amount of time
each week to see if any of your plants need some attention.

This book starts in early spring and ends with late winter. Although early
spring is the best time to start gardening, you can begin at any time during
the year.

Gardening is about sharing – sharing the space with plants and animals,
and sharing the garden with your family and friends.

Good luck with your growing!

Spring

Early Spring

What's going on in the garden?

Spring is coming. Snowdrops are pushing through the ground.
The days are getting longer and it's becoming warmer
in the garden. Animals that went into hibernation to avoid
a cold, hungry winter are starting to wake up now. Insects are hatching
from eggs or changing from larvae or pupae into their adult forms
to face the new season. Birds are getting ready to build their nests
and this is the best time of year to attract them to your garden.

Nest boxes

If you set up a nest box in your garden it will encourage birds to nest there, and you might be able to see them raise their young.

It is important to choose the best type of box for the birds you want to attract. Open-fronted boxes are best for robins and wrens, while boxes with small holes are good for tits and flycatchers. There are even really big boxes with very big holes for owls and special cup-shaped boxes to attach under the roof for house martins and swallows.

You can buy a nest box from your garden centre. Place the box out of the reach of cats, and in a south-west facing position, if possible, to make it attractive to the birds.

Birdsong

While you're in the garden you can listen out for the calls of the birds around you. Keep a notebook handy and start writing down, or drawing all the birds that visit your garden. You will soon be able to recognise their different calls.

15

What's happening to the plants?

The first leaf-buds on trees and shrubs (like sycamore and hawthorn) are starting to burst. These plants have a head start on herbaceous (non-woody) plants because their woody structures have been there all winter and don't have to grow every spring from ground level. Crocuses and daffodils *(see right)*, which grow from corms or bulbs, are also beginning to flower – the bulb is a swollen food store that gives the new growth a real boost. This is why it's a good idea to plant lots of bulbs in autumn. They will flower early and bring colour to the garden when many other plants have hardly started to appear.

What can I do in the garden?

Sow Seeds Indoors

It's still too early to sow seeds outside in the garden – the soil isn't warm enough and they won't germinate well. But you can make a start by sowing some seeds indoors, in your house or in a greenhouse. You can then move them outside in a few weeks' time, when they have grown into young plants (see page 25). Choose hardy plants at this stage (like candytuft or lettuce), because there is still a risk of frost damage if the weather is cold.

You will need

• **seed compost** – you need the sort of compost that is sold especially for seeds, sometimes called 'seed and cutting compost'.

• **a propagator** – this is a pot, tray or other container with holes in the bottom for drainage and with a cover to stop the compost from drying out. You can buy a small plastic tray-style propagator with a clear firm plastic lid, or you can use an ordinary plant pot with a plastic bag attached to the top with an elastic band.

1. Fill the pots or propagator with compost and then very gently press it down.

2. Sow your seeds. Some types of seed should be scattered on the surface of the compost, but others need a light layer of compost on top – check your seed packet.

3. Water the seeds. It's best to do this with a fine mist sprayer as you don't want to drown your seeds. Under the plastic cover, the compost won't dry out and you shouldn't need to water again until the seedlings have appeared.

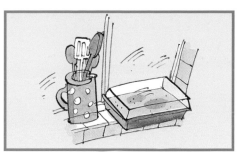

4. Place the pots or propagator somewhere light but not too hot – a partly shaded windowsill is good.

5. It will take one to three weeks for your seeds to germinate, and then your first seedlings will peep above the compost *(see below)*. Make a few holes in the propagator cover or open the vents to let in some fresh air.

Pruning

If your garden has flowering shrubs like roses *(see right)*, berberis or hydrangeas they will need special care at this time of year if they are to flower well. You need to cut back parts of the plant to make a neat and tidy shape and help it to put all its strength into producing flowers instead of leaves. This is called pruning. The easiest types of shrub to prune are large-flowered roses, so you could start with these if you have them in your garden.

You will need

• a pair of pruners or secateurs (which are like very strong scissors – ask an adult to help you at first)

• gloves (if your roses are very prickly)

1. Cut any dead or feeble shoots right back to the base of the shrub.

2. Cut all the other shoots down to half their height, making your cut just above a bud – the buds appear as small swellings on the shoots.

3. Chop up the pieces you cut off and take them to the compost bin. (see page 81).

Make it! Bird table

You will need

- An old wooden or plastic tray
- two pieces of nylon cord, each about 2 metres long

1. Ask an adult to punch a hole at each corner of the tray, plus six more holes all around the tray for rainwater to drain away.

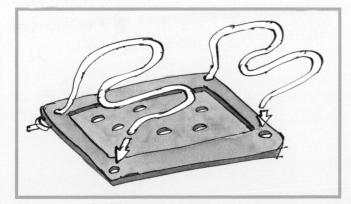

2. Take one of the pieces of cord and thread it through one of the corner holes. Tie a big knot to fix it. Do the same with the second piece of cord at the other end of the tray.

3. Ask an adult to help you hang your tray on a branch or a post – high enough to be out of the reach of cats, but low enough for you to reach.

19

Mid Spring

What's going on in the garden?

Spring has really arrived now, and birds are beginning to build their nests. If you were able to put up a nest box last month, the birds might now be using it.

Birds and mammals are warm-blooded, which means they can produce their own body heat. But other animals can't do this and they only begin to be active when it gets warmer outside.

Slugs and Snails

Slugs and snails are coming out now, and it's exciting to go looking for them in your garden after dark. Take a torch and you will be amazed at the number you find.

Gardeners often collect up snails and slugs to remove them, and if they are eating your plants this is a good idea. But most kinds of slug and snail are harmless to plants, for example the gigantic Great Black Slug, the biggest of all our British slugs. It can be 20 centimetres long, and despite its name it is sometimes bright orange!

Wasps

Some of the first insects to appear are large wasps. They are the queens which have been hibernating during the winter. They have been carrying eggs since the autumn and are now ready to find a suitable hole to build a nest. The eggs hatch into worker wasps *(see left)* which then take over the job of enlarging the nest to make room for more eggs. By mid summer the nest may contain over 20,000 insects and the worker wasps catch many garden pests to feed the young!

21

What's happening to the plants?

Containers

The bulbs you planted in the autumn
(see page 83) will be growing nicely in your
containers now. Growing plants in containers
is a good idea as they can be placed in parts of
the garden where there is no soil, or you
can put them in a courtyard or patio, or on a
windowsill. If the flowers fade in one pot, you
can move it away and put another in its place.
You can make plant containers from old tubs
and cans, but they must have drainage holes
in the bottom for water to run away. Tubs and
window boxes are very easy to plant up, but
make sure you use fresh compost in them
each spring. Old compost will have very little
fertiliser and may contain pests and diseases.

Lawns

Lawns are found in many gardens,
even small ones. They are
wonderful areas to play on, but
they also help to create a frame
for your garden around which
you can arrange the other plants.
The type of grass to use on lawns
is especially chosen to be hard-
wearing. Lawns can be grown
from seed, but it is quicker and
easier to buy turf. This is 'ready-
made' lawn and is dug up and
rolled in strips like carpet.

What can I do in the garden?

Sow seeds outdoors

Now the soil is beginning to warm up, you can sow seeds directly into the garden. But choose smaller seeds like pot marigolds, candytuft, larkspur or lettuce *(see right)*, because if the weather suddenly gets cold again, it's the biggest seeds that suffer most. Peas and beans are very vulnerable to cold, so wait a while to plant these.

You will need
- a garden fork
- fertiliser
- rubber gloves
- seeds
- a rake

1. Choose a warm and sunny place – not too big an area – about 2 x 3 metres is easy to manage.

2. Dig the bed with a fork to remove weeds, large stones and hard clods of soil.

3. Rake the soil level and remove smaller stones.

23

4. Scatter some fertiliser and carefully rake this in too. Always wear rubber gloves when you are handling fertiliser.

5. For vegetable seeds, make a shallow groove by dragging a stick along the surface of the soil. This is called a drill. If you can't reach to do this without treading on the soil, put down a plank and stand on that – it will prevent the newly-raked soil from being flattened.

6. Tear across the top of your seed packet and gently tap it so the seeds fall out into the drill. The bigger the seeds, the further apart they should be placed, but make sure none are actually touching each other. If you do sow too many, you can pull out the extra seedlings later.

7. Carefully push the soil back over the seeds with the rake and gently press it down.

For flower seeds, sprinkle the seeds over the soil in small groups and carefully rake them so they are slightly buried.

Plant outdoors – transplanting

The seeds you sowed indoors (see page 16) should now have germinated, and soon the plants will be big enough to go outside. This is called transplanting. Most types of plant should be at least 5 centimetres tall before you do this, and first you must get them used to colder conditions. This is called 'hardening off'. The seedlings from indoors have been living a very cosy, snug life and aren't quite tough enough for the garden. You can harden them off by putting the seed trays and pots outside in the daytime and taking them in at night for about ten days.

You will need

- a trowel
- a watering can
- labels and a pencil

1. Prepare the planting position in the garden in the same way you did for seeds, though the soil doesn't need to be raked quite as finely.

3. Make a small hole in the soil with your fingers or a trowel and gently push the new plant into it.

4. Carefully press down the soil around the plant with your fingers, and gently water it.

5. Add a label to remind you what the plant is. Then wash your hands!

2. Carefully remove the young plant from its seed tray with a clump of compost still around the roots – you can use an old kitchen fork for this.

Plant seed potatoes

You can plant potatoes outside now. It's very easy and they will begin to grow almost before you know it. Potatoes are good plants to grow in a new garden because they have so much leafy growth they smother weeds. See page 76 to find out how to dig your potatoes when they are ready.

You will need

- seed potatoes
- fertiliser
- rubber gloves
- a trowel
- a rake

1. Buy a bag of seed potatoes from the garden centre. They look the same as potatoes from the supermarket but they have been grown especially for planting.

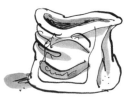

2. Dig the soil, adding some fertiliser. The soil doesn't need to be dug as carefully as it does for seeds.

3. Plant the potatoes with a trowel, about 40 centimetres apart and 15 centimetres deep.

4. As soon as the shoots poke above the soil surface, rake some soil into a ridge over them to protect them from frost.

Sow sprouting seeds

It's great fun to sow some seeds in a glass jar so you can watch what is happening when they germinate. Choose big seeds like broad beans so you can see clearly what's going on.

You will need

- broad bean seeds
- a clean jar
- absorbent paper
- sand

1. Soak three broad bean seeds for a few hours in water.

2. Place a tube of absorbent paper inside your glass jar. Kitchen roll is ideal.

3. Pour sand into the tube so the paper is pushed against the sides of the jar.

4. Push the seeds carefully between the absorbent paper and the side of the jar, making sure the seeds are about halfway down and at least 5 centimetres apart.

5. Carefully pour water on to the sand until the sand and paper become soaked through.

6. Put the jar in a well-lit place such as on a windowsill, turning it every few days and topping up the water if the paper starts to dry out. After a few days you should see the root start to grow downwards and then later, the shoot growing upwards.

Plant hanging baskets

Hanging baskets are fun to plant, but you will need to water them very frequently. Good plants to choose for a hanging basket are petunias, lobelias and pansies.

You will need

- a hanging basket
- compost
- soft liner
- plants

1. Choose a basket made of green plastic-coated wire, about 30 centimetres in diameter.

2. Line the basket. There are several types of liner, but the soft kinds made from wool or other fibres are best.

3. Fill the bottom of the basket with hanging basket compost.

4. Carefully remove the young plants from their tray or pots. Choose the strongest plants you can find.

5. Starting from the inside of the basket, gently work some of the plants through the wire at the bottom of the basket so that the roots are inside and the plants hang below.

6. Add a layer of compost and then another layer of plants. This time, arrange the plants so they are poking through the sides of the basket.

7. Fill the rest of the basket with compost, add your top layer of plants and water thoroughly.

Make it! Flower pot presents

It's great to make your own gifts for Easter and birthdays – and you can find some lovely ideas in the garden. Why not decorate a pretty flower pot to show off some of your spring bulbs?

You will need

- silver foil
- tissue paper
- daffodils or crocuses in pots
- glue

1. Carefully dig up a few daffodils or crocuses that have grown from the bulbs you planted in the autumn (see page 83). They will just be shoots at the moment but soon flowers will start to form.

2. Plant them in a pot with some compost and bring them into the light and warmth of your home.

3. Cover the top of the pot with silver foil and decorate it: glue shapes of tissue paper to match the colour of your flowers.

Late Spring

What's going on in the garden?

Birds are now feeding their babies and if you use the correct kind of food (such as sunflower seeds or specially prepared mixtures) on your bird table, you can help them. You shouldn't use kitchen scraps as some may be harmful. As the young birds begin to leave their nests they are most at risk from enemies, including our pets! It's an amazing fact that more than 275 million wild creatures are killed each year in Britain by the 9 million domestic cats.

You could put a collar with a bell on your cat to help warn the birds.

Many summer-visiting birds arrive in the garden at this time of year. Cuckoos are in the nearby countryside, and you may hear their call. But they are very shy, so you will be lucky to see one. The sky will be full of swallows, martins and swifts, and you can watch them wheel and turn, catching insects as they fly.

Pond Life

A pond is a great way to see a huge variety of wonderful wildlife. Perhaps you have one in your garden or at your school. Remember that ponds can be dangerous places, and you should only go close to the edge of a pond if an adult is with you.

Pond dipping is great fun. Attach a jar to the end of a pole. Dip it into the water, and collect a small amount of water from the pond. Look at it closely – a magnifying glass will help. You will see masses of tiny creatures swimming and wriggling in the water. Many of them are insect larvae which hatch into flying adults when the weather gets warmer.

If you don't have a pond, leave a clean jar in the garden. As it fills with rainwater, you may see the insect larvae swimming around in the jar.

Frogs

A pond can be a great haven for frogs. You are most likely to see one when it is disturbed among the plants at the pond's edge and hops into the water. If you are lucky, frogs may lay their spawn in your pond. Then you can watch the spawn hatch into tadpoles and finally turn into baby frogs. If your pond has a firm and hard edge of stone slabs, lay a piece of wood or stone to make a slope, so the baby frogs can easily climb out on to dry land when they are old enough.

Newts

You are most likely to see newts in the water when they swim up to the surface. Newts may breed in your pond, but they lay their eggs singly on water plants, not in large masses like frogs. They also hatch into tadpoles and leave the water later in the year.

What's happening to the plants?

Late spring is the busiest time of year for gardeners, when plants are growing quickly in the garden. The plants which are still indoors are becoming too big for their pots and seed trays and need to be transplanted as soon as possible.

It isn't just the plants that are growing quickly. Weeds are appearing as if by magic. Some, such as groundsel and shepherd's purse, are annuals that have grown from seed this year, just like the garden seeds. But others, like thistles, nettles and bindweed *(see right)* are perennials which produce new shoots every season from their roots deep in the soil. They grow so quickly that they will choke your garden plants if you don't stop them – after all, they grow in the garden naturally, and it is your plants which are intruding into their home!

Weeding

Weeding simply means controlling the weeds. You can pull out annual weeds by hand. Or, if there are a lot of weeds, use a hoe. A Dutch hoe is a tool with a long handle that is used to slice off the weeds. It's important to do this on a hot, dry day so that the weeds shrivel quickly. If you hoe when the ground is wet, they will simply start growing again.

Perennial weeds are often too deeply rooted to pull out, though sometimes you can dig them out with a fork. You can chop them off with a hoe to make the garden look tidy, but they will grow again from their strong, deep roots.

Sow half-hardy plants

There is very little risk of frost now, so you can sow and plant the kinds of plants we call 'half-hardy'. These all come from warmer climates and will grow outside in the summer, but can't stand the cold. This type of plant includes pelargoniums *(see above left)* and fuschias *(see above right)*. Many half-hardy plants are very fast-growing.

What can I do in the garden?

Plant runner beans

1. Choose an area of about 1.5 x 1.5 metres and prepare the soil just as you do for other seeds (see page 23).

2. Push in the bamboo canes in a circle. The canes should be about 20 centimetres apart. Tie them together at the top.

3. Wrap some garden string around the outside to make a wigwam. There should be about 20 centimetres between each ring of string.

You will need

- long bamboo canes
- runner bean seeds
- a ball of garden string

4. Push in two runner bean seeds at the base of each cane. You might like to choose two or three varieties with different coloured flowers – white, red or pink – to produce an attractive effect.

5. Pull out the smaller seedling of each pair if both of them germinate to give the best one room to grow.

6. As the plants grow, their shoots will gradually twine around the canes and soon flowers and delicious beans will form. Keep the plants well watered.

7. Pick your beans regularly to encourage new pods to grow.

Plant sunflowers

See if you can beat the sunflower record. The tallest was over seven metres high! Buy a packet of sunflower seeds – if you want a record-breaking plant, be sure to choose a tall variety and not one of the dwarf kinds.

1. Choose a sunny spot in the garden and dig in plenty of compost and a little fertiliser.

2. Push in two or three seeds and if they all germinate, choose the biggest one to keep and pull out the others.

3. Push in a bamboo cane next to your plant and keep it well watered.

4. As the stem grows, tie it carefully to the cane.

You will need

- sunflower seeds
- a strong bamboo cane
- liquid fertiliser

5. If you give your plant some liquid tomato fertiliser once a week (see page 53), you will have a taller plant – and you might just break that record!

Sow pumpkins and marrows

You will only need one or two plants as they grow very large very quickly.

3. Keep the plant well watered, look for the lovely yellow flowers – and then watch your giant fruit develop.

1. Choose an area about 1 metre x 1 metre and dig in lots of compost and a little fertiliser – these plants like really lush soil conditions.

2. Sow two seeds of your pumpkin or marrow close together. It's best to push them in sideways, and if both germinate, pull out the weaker seedling.

Sow nasturtiums

Nasturtiums *(see right)* thrive in poor soil. Scatter some seeds in a sunny spot and use a rake to lightly cover them. They will flower all summer long. The flowers are in glorious shades of orange, red, yellow and cream – and they are edible! They have a lovely spicy taste in summer salads. Remember some plants are poisonous. Always check with an adult before eating anything from the garden.

Make it! Egg-heads

You can use eggs to make egg-head gardens!
You might like to make a separate egg
garden for each member of your family!

You will need
- hard-boiled eggs
- cotton wool
- cress or mustard seeds

1. Paint faces on the shells of hard-boiled eggs.

2. Slice off the tops and scoop out the egg.

3. Fill the empty shells with cotton wool.

4. Sprinkle some cress or mustard seeds
on top of the cotton wool and moisten
well.

5. Cover the seeds with a small
pad of moist cotton wool and put
the egg in a warm place.

6. As soon as the seeds germinate,
remove the cotton wool pad and
allow the green 'hair' to stand up.

SPRING – CHECK IT!

Have you done everything in spring to help your garden get ready for the warm summer months? Here is a checklist of the activities we have talked about this season. We have also included a guide to what plants will be flowering in spring, to add colour to your garden while you grow your plants.

Have you...

☐ Sown indoor seedlings?

☐ Pruned your large shrubs?

☐ Grown a plant in a pot?

☐ Sown vegetable and flower seeds?

☐ Transplanted your indoor seedlings?

☐ Planted seed potatoes?

☐ Sown bean seeds in a glass jar?

☐ Made a hanging basket?

☐ Weeded your garden?

☐ Sown half-hardy plants?

☐ Made a runner-bean wigwam?

☐ Planted a sunflower?

☐ Planted a pumpkin seed?

☐ Sown nasturtiums?

☐ Made an egg-head garden?

Top plants that flower in spring

Welsh Poppy

Crocus

Daffodil

Tulip

Snowdrop

Lily of the Valley

Hyacinth

Primrose

summer

Early Summer

What's going on in the garden?

People often talk about the 'hum' of the fields and gardens in summer and if you sit still and listen, you will hear what they mean. Insects are everywhere, humming, buzzing – and generally being busy. But what are all these thousands of insects doing as they flit from flower to flower? They are collecting nectar and pollen to eat and feed to their young. Nectar is a sweet fluid produced by flowers, and pollen is the fine yellow powder that is passed from flower to flower to produce seeds. This is the reason why many flowers are brightly coloured or beautifully perfumed. They need to attract insects for pollination.

When an insect visits a flower, some of the pollen sticks to its body. It carries this to the next flower and the pollen fertilises it. Bees are the most important insects for pollinating flowers in our gardens. In some tropical climates, other creatures also pollinate flowers – humming birds, bats (which pollinate flowers that open at night), even slugs pollinate flowers that are formed at soil level!

Mice and voles

Many wild animals need our protection. Usually this is because their natural habitat has been destroyed, or their natural food is no longer available. Two animals that don't need protection, however, are mice and voles (except for the rare water vole). It's thought that there are over 70 million voles in Britain! They can cause trouble in gardens because they feed on stored fruit and vegetables and take the seeds that we have sown. So make sure there are no tiny holes in sheds and other storage places and put wire netting or other protection over valuable plants and seeds.

Bats

Did you know that there are more kinds of bat in Britain than any other kind of mammal? We have about sixteen different types and all must be protected. It is against the law to harm bats or to disturb the places where they roost. Bats are important animals in gardens because they eat large numbers of harmful insects. If you sit in your garden just as it is beginning to get dark, you will almost certainly see one or two bats swooping over the lawn, catching gnats and mosquitoes as they fly. They will probably be pipistrelles as these are the commonest and the smallest British species. Putting a bat box up is a good way to help bats. Good ones can be found at garden centres or from organisations like the Royal Society for the Protection of Birds (RSPB). Get an adult to place your box as high as possible on a building or tree and make sure there is enough room for bats to fly in.

What's happening to the plants?

Your perennial plants will be in flower by now, but the first of this season's annual flowers have also started to appear, like sweet peas *(see right)*. These annuals have grown quickly since the seeds were sown, and vegetable seedlings that were still in the packet a few weeks ago are now growing vigorously. The garden has a feeling of excitement everywhere.

Mowing the lawn

Lawn-mowing is one of the regular gardening tasks in summer. Grass is an unusual plant because the new leaves grow from the bottom so you can mow it without damaging the cells that produce the new growth. Most plants grow from the top and if they were mown, the special cells would be cut off – so you wouldn't produce a very good lawn from Michaelmas daisies!

Have you ever wondered how gardeners manage to produce the attractive stripes on lawns and football pitches? They use a *cylinder* mower. As the mower is pushed up and down, the blades push the grass first one way and then the other. The light reflecting off the grass in different ways gives the striped effect. Other mowers are called *rotary*. These have whirling blades that slash the grass.

It's fun to help with lawn-mowing but you should never use any garden machinery unless an adult is present. Always wear strong shoes to protect your feet from the sharp blades.

44

Weeding your lawn

Small numbers of daisies in the lawn can look very pretty, but if there are too many, the best way to keep them under control is to use a daisy-grubber to dig them out. Use a mower with a collector box to ensure weed seeds and cuttings aren't spread everywhere.

Globe-trotting plants

Some of the plants we grow in our gardens are British species that grow here naturally – we call them native species. Many plants, however, have been brought to this country from other parts of the world by plant collectors and explorers. They collected the seeds on their travels and brought them back to Europe. Two of these plants, found in many British gardens, are runner beans and pelargoniums.

Runner beans (*see left*) grow wild in Central America and when the seeds were brought to Britain nearly 400 years ago, people grew them for their coloured flowers. It wasn't until 100 years later that they were first grown as vegetables. You might have planted a runner-bean wigwam in spring (see page 35). If you didn't, it's not too late to sow some beans. There are types with red, white, pink and red-and-white flowers.

Pelargoniums (*see right*) grow wild in South Africa. The sailing ships of the East India Company called there on their way home from trading in the Far East and first brought them to Europe around 300 years ago. Plants from hot areas with little rainfall make good choices as summer flowers because they thrive in warm sunny weather and are used to dry conditions. They don't need someone to water them while you are on holiday!

45

What can I do in the garden?

Dead-heading

Some flowers last for many weeks while others only look good for a day or two before they turn brown or fade. On some annual flowers, like petunias, you can simply pull off the dead flower head with your fingers. Other plants need a trim to keep them healthy and happy. This is called dead-heading. We do this to make the plant look neater but it also prevents diseases attacking the dead blossom and spreading to the rest of the plant. It also encourages new flowers to open.

You will need

- pruners or secateurs
- gloves
- a bucket to put the dead flowers into

1. Look carefully for the flowers that are fading or turning brown.

2. Carefully trace the stalk back to where you can see fresh green leaves.

3. Use your pruners to snip just above the green leaf.

4. Put the dead flowers in a bucket to be added to your compost bin (see page 81).

Sow seeds in succession

Although it's great to see your vegetables growing from the seeds you have sown, it's also annoying if the crops are all ready at the same time and don't last through the summer. An important trick to learn is to sow a few at a time. This is called 'sowing in succession'. Lettuces are the best vegetables to start practising with. Sow a few more seeds as soon as the baby seedlings from the last sowing are appearing above the soil.

You will need

- a stick to make a drill
- a rake
- seeds

1. Make sure you have room in your sowing bed for several rows of seeds each about 1 metre long and half a metre apart.

2. Sow a row of seeds (see page 23).

4. Now sow the second row.

3. After about ten days, look out for the first signs of green seedling leaves peeping above the soil.

5. Continue sowing seeds at 10-day intervals until you have filled your sowing bed. By the time you sow the last row, you will probably have eaten the plants you sowed first!

Plant a herb garden

Herbs are plants such as parsley, basil or thyme, that are used in cooking to add flavour. They are easy to grow and herbs picked fresh from the garden taste better than those bought at a shop. They can be grown in a small bed close to the kitchen or in pots. You can also grow herbs in small pots on a window-sill indoors and this is useful in winter when it's too cold for them outside. You can easily look after perennial herbs like thyme and sage all year in this way. You can also grow herbs like parsley and basil that are raised from seeds every year. It's best to use one small pot for each kind of herb but group them together in a larger shallow pot to make an attractive herb garden.

1. Plant the small perennial herb plants in your pots.

You will need

- pots
- strong perennial herb plants
- annual herb seeds
- potting compost

3. Herbs need almost no fertiliser but will need watering every few days.

2. Scatter annual herb seeds on to potting compost. Sprinkle a little of the compost on top.

Make it! Dried herbs

The best time to dry herbs is just before they flower. This method works well with woody herbs like rosemary and thyme but it won't work so well with herbs like basil or parsley.

You will need:

- a pair of scissors
- kitchen roll
- paper bags
- pencil
- string

1. Use your scissors to snip off stems from your plant. Make sure you remove any leaves that are turning brown.

2. Rinse your cuttings in cold water and carefully dry them with some kitchen roll. This is important as wet herbs may go mouldy.

4. Tie five or six stems together in a small bundle with some string and put the bundle upside down into the paper bag.

5. Gather the bag around the stems and tie it with more string.

6. Hang up the bag in an airing cupboard or a warm room.

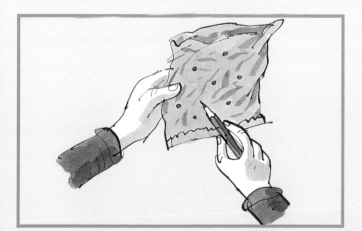

3. Take a paper bag and punch some holes through the sides with a pencil. This is to allow air to circulate through the bag. Write the name of the herb you are drying on the bag.

7. After three weeks, check the leaves to make sure they are drying nicely and are not going mouldy. The herbs should be ready in 4–6 weeks.

Mid Summer

What's going on in the garden?

Butterflies are among the most beautiful visitors to our gardens. Some species are rare because their natural habitats and their food plants are being lost or damaged as a result of new building, farming and other land development. We can help by making our gardens as attractive to butterflies as possible. Butterflies like nectar-rich plants such as buddleja and Michaelmas daisies. These can be planted at any time of the year if you buy the plants in containers. Buddleja is a fairly big shrub so it will need an area of at least 1 metre to grow. It's not at all unusual to find as many as five different kinds of butterfly on a buddleja bush at the same time.

Look out for red admiral, painted lady, small tortoiseshell (*see right*), comma, peacock, large and small whites, green-veined white, holly blue and meadow brown butterflies.

If you want butterflies to lay eggs and produce caterpillars, you also need some plants to provide food for them when they hatch. Stinging nettles are the food plant of many butterflies, so you could keep a small clump of them in the garden.

Moths can be beautiful too and you may see a fascinating insect that is becoming commoner in our gardens as summers get warmer. The hummingbird hawk-moth looks just like a small humming bird as it hovers in front of flowers, drinking nectar with its long tongue. It is especially fond of pelargoniums.

Watching the weather

Gardeners always talk about the weather. This is because they need to know what will be happening so they can plan their gardening properly. Knowing exactly what the weather will be doing is difficult, but television weather forecasts can be very useful.

You can measure the amount of rain that falls on your garden by using a bottle with a funnel on top. If you mark the bottle in centimetres, write down the results and empty it each week, you can compare the amount of rain that falls in your garden throughout the year.

51

What's happening to the plants?

If it is hot and sunny and hasn't rained for a while, the garden will start to look a bit dry. You will need to think about watering your plants. Water is a precious substance. Although there are many kinds of hosepipes and sprinklers for watering the garden, you should only use water where it is really needed. Plants in pots and tubs are the most important to water as the compost in the pots dries out quickly. Then you should water your annual plants in the beds and borders.

Do not waste water on the lawn. Even in a really hot, dry summer when the lawn is brown and looks dead, it will always come to life again after rain has fallen.

Mid summer is a great time for seeing everything at its best. Nearly all the flowers and flowering shrubs are at their most colourful. This is because the annuals you sowed in the spring have grown quickly and have caught up with the plants that have been in the garden since last year. Some of the fastest growing annuals are the sunflowers you sowed (see page 36). They can become more than 5 metres tall in just a few months. Their huge flowers turn slowly thoughout the day and always follow the sun across the sky (*see right*).

What can I do in the garden?

Feed your plants

Plants need extra care now. They are growing so strongly and quickly – they are using food and water very fast. This is the time of year to use liquid feed as it is soaked up by the plant much faster than a dry powder. Tomato fertiliser is a good choice. You can buy it from your local garden centre.

You will need:
- a watering can
- tomato fertiliser

1. According to the instructions on the bottle, mix the fertiliser in a watering can full of water.

2. Water each plant that you want to feed. Make sure the soil around each plant is thoroughly soaked.

Grow tomatoes

Tomatoes are great fun to grow, but they can't be planted out in the garden until the summer because they are tender plants. One of the best varieties to grow is *Gardeners' Delight* which produces lots of tiny tomatoes.

If you want to raise your own plants from seeds, you will need to sow them in early spring (see page 16). However as you will only want three or four plants it may be easier to buy them at your garden centre. The plants can be grown in the garden or in a pot. They are also often grown in special bags of compost called growing-bags which can be bought at your garden centre.

You will need

- two or three tomato plants
- a growing-bag
- scissors or a knife – get an adult to help you with this.
- a watering can

1. Lay the growing-bag on its side and cut large slits in the top.

2. Place the base of the plants gently through the slits and into the compost so the roots are buried but the leaves and stem are poking out of the bag.

3. Water the plant well. It's important to keep tomatoes well watered and also to give them special tomato fertiliser once a week (see page 53).

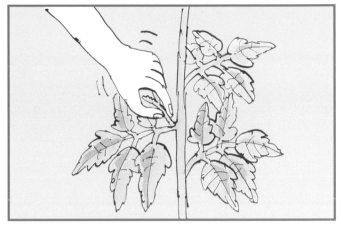

4. As your plants get bigger you will have to prune them in a special way. It is called side-shooting. Use your finger and thumb to pinch off any branches that grow from the main stem. If you don't do this, the plant will become a tangled mass and won't produce many tomatoes.

5. Pick your fruit when they are bright red. Don't eat them all before you get back to the kitchen!

Thinning

Some of the annual flowers and vegetables that you sowed in the ground in the spring may now be growing in really thick clumps. This is because you sprinkled too many seeds at once and the plants will be fighting against each other to survive. All you have to do is pull out some of the young plants so there are a few centimetres of soil between each plant. This is called thinning. It seems wasteful but is necessary to be sure you get the best results.

Check your fruit and vegetables

Some of the vegetables in the kitchen garden are ripening now but it isn't always easy to tell exactly when each kind is ready to eat.

Cabbages and lettuces

Gently feel the head of the plant with your fingers. If it is firm, it is ready. If it is still soft and squashy, leave it for a little while longer.

Carrots and beetroot

These are difficult to check. It is best to pull up one or two. If they are ready, the top part of the vegetable should be bulging above the soil surface and feel firm.

Soft fruit (currants, raspberries, gooseberries and strawberries)

These should be fully coloured before they are picked. Don't pick them when they are green.

Make it! Pot-pourri

It's sad that most garden flowers last for such a short time. One day they are beautiful and sweet smelling and then only a few days later they can be brown and faded – just like dead leaves. But we can make them last a little longer. Pot-pourri is a sweet-smelling collection of dried flowers or flower petals that is put inside a house. It's easy to make pot-pourri but you need to pick the flowers when they are fully open and fresh, not as they are starting to fade. Make sure your parents don't mind if you collect some – and don't collect every flower in your garden! The very best flowers to collect are roses and lavender because they are still sweet smelling after they have dried. Collect a few others like marigolds and cornflowers to add bright colours.

You will need:

- flower petals
- a baking tray and wire rack
- a bowl for display

1. Choose a warm dry day to collect your petals.

2. Put them on a wire rack in a baking tin.

4. After about a week, they will be dry and the smell will be even better if you add a little cinnamon and a few drops of rose oil which can be bought at health food shops.

3. Place in the airing cupboard or a very warm part of your home.

5. Put your pot-pourri in an open bowl. Everyone will love the fresh smell of your summer garden!

Late Summer

What's going on in the garden?

As we come towards the second half of summer, lots of the plants we have been looking after during the season are at last beginning to reward us for all our work! And many gardeners think the biggest reward comes from fruit trees and bushes. The best fruit comes at the end of the season with blackberries. It's very hard not to eat more than you put in your basket! If you don't have any fruit plants in your garden, you can still collect blackberries from wild plants in the hedgerows – and they may taste even better. Make sure you always have an adult with you. It's a good idea to wear old clothes too because blackberry juice has a habit of making large red stains!

The global greenhouse

Changes to the environment all over the world mean that the weather is warmer than it was when our parents and grandparents were children. In many places it is now unusual to see snow in winter and there are often long periods in the summer without rain. This has an effect on our gardens because many of the flowers that have been popular in gardens in the past – like lupins and delphiniums – are harder to grow unless they are watered very frequently. Perhaps in the future it would be better to choose plants like pelargoniums and gazanias (*see right*) that come from warmer areas and are better able to cope with the warmer, drier conditions.

Looking at other gardens

Why not visit some of the gardens that are open to the public? You will recognise many of the plants but often these gardens are very large so they may include great lakes, buildings and many huge trees. You will see the way that people have used ideas they have copied from all over the world – like Japanese and Chinese gardens. You may want to take pictures of the plants you like best. Be inspired by these beautiful places and perhaps try to recreate the things you like in your own garden!

What's happening to the plants?

The flower garden may look a bit sad at this time of year. Many of the flowers that have been brightening our gardens over the summer are coming to the end of their display. Others may have a white mould called mildew or other disease on the leaves, making them appear ragged *(see left)*. This shows how important it is to have different kinds of plants in your garden. Your trees and shrubs will still be looking good.

Rock plants

If you look at walls and rocks near to where you live, you will see many plants living very happily on them – it's often hard even to see any soil. Many are tiny things like mosses and small ferns but sometimes really large plants, such as wallflowers, manage to grow well too. They aren't really growing without any soil, but they only need a very small amount of it and if we have walls in our gardens, we should make use of them too. The best plants to grow in this way are those called alpines or rock garden plants. If you don't have a wall in your garden, you can plant them in pots or in the cracks between paving slabs – some of them don't even mind being walked on!

Alpines should be grown in pots of compost that is similar to the soil in the mountains. You can buy small alpine plants like thymes and push their roots into the cracks in paving or walls to grow, but it can be difficult to get them started. You might also like to try mixing some seeds with potting compost and brushing or pushing this into cracks too.

What can I do in the garden?

Check fruit trees or bushes

It is now time to check the fruit trees in your garden. Different varieties of fruit grow at different speeds and ripen at different times, but apples, pears *(see below)* and plums *(see right)* will all be ripening about now. If your garden is too small for more than one tree, choose a family apple tree for your garden. This is a tree with two or three different varieties grafted or made to grow on the same stem. These different varieties will all ripen at slightly different times. Fruit trees are best planted in late autumn or early winter (see page 91). You can tell when apples are ripe because if you gently lift the fruit with your hand, its stalk will snap away from the tree.

Some other kinds of fruit have varieties that ripen at different times too. Raspberries are good examples. If you choose an autumn variety of raspberries, you will find they are ripening about now – at a time when most people no longer have any raspberries left.

Collect seeds

Some of the best plants for collecting seeds are nasturtiums (*see right*), poppies and pot marigolds, as they produce plenty of seeds and these are perfect to collect and sow next year. Remember that you must collect your seeds before the first frosts otherwise they may be damaged.

You will need:

- pruners or scissors
- paper bags or envelopes
- a pencil

1. Once the flowers on your plant have faded, you will see the seed pods begin to form.

3. Leave the bags open at the top and keep them somewhere dry for the seeds to ripen. They will then fall from the pods or they can be gently rubbed out.

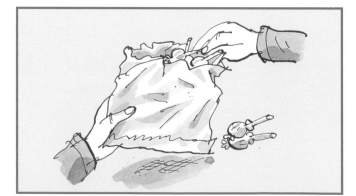

2. Carefully cut some stems from the plants with seed pods attached and place them in paper bags. You must not use plastic bags because the seeds will rot.

4. Keep them in paper envelopes until the spring when you can sow them. Don't forget to write the names of your seeds on the packet.

Sow seeds for autumn

We always have to plan ahead in the garden. In the spring we had to think ahead to the summer and make sure our seeds were sown in time to produce flowers and vegetables. But seed-sowing doesn't stop in the spring. If you want fresh parsley and salad leaves during the winter months, you should sow them now. You could sow a mixture of curly parsley which looks very pretty, and broad-leaved parsley which has a better flavour. Lettuces aren't very reliable in the winter but a spicy plant that is well worth growing to add to salads is winter cress. This is a tough plant that can survive the cold winter months. Sow a short row near to your parsley – and close to the kitchen. Try a row of quick-growing radish too (*see above right*).

You will need

- a stick to make a drill
- your chosen seeds in packets
- a watering can

1. Make a seed drill about 60 centimetres long (see page 24) in a sunny part of the garden.

3. If the weather is dry, give the seeds a little water from your watering can.

2. Scatter seeds thinly along the drill. Gently push back the soil and press it down.

4. Pick a few leaves from each winter cress plant when they are well grown so more will come.

Take cuttings

Not all garden plants are grown from seeds. Some have been bred by nurseries in a special way and aren't able to produce seeds. So how do we get new young plants without seeds? We take cuttings. Late summer is a good time to take cuttings from plants such as fuschias and pelargoniums *(see right)*.

You will need

- pruners or scissors
- a propagator (see page 16)
- seed compost

1. Cut one or two stems from your plants and then use a knife to cut them into shorter lengths. Be careful and make sure an adult is watching you. Make sure that each length has at least one bud and one leaf on it.

2. Gently push the stem into the compost. Make sure the green leafy part is at the top about 2 centimetres above the soil level.

3. Water very gently using a mist sprayer.

5. Check the cuttings every week and when you see new leaves appearing, you will know they are making roots and becoming new plants.

4. Place the cover over the propagator and keep it somewhere fairly warm.

6. About three weeks after the first leaves appear, you can gently dig them up and put them into their own pots of compost. Again, make sure they are well watered.

Make it! Pressed flower pictures

These make lovely presents for family and friends to remind them of your garden.

You will need:

- a photograph or picture frame
- a flower press or absorbent paper and a heavy book
- card
- flowers and leaves
- glue
- cocktail sticks

3. Measure the card to fit your frame. Choose the flowers and leaves which have dried the best and carefully arrange them to create the effect you want.

4. Carefully glue each flower and leaf in place using tiny blobs of clear glue on a cocktail stick.

1. Choose flowers that are brightly coloured and not too thick and fleshy – also a few attractive leaves such as ivy and ferns. Collect the flowers and leaves and dry them in a flower press or between layers of blotting paper or newspaper with a heavy book on top.

2. Leave them in a warm dry place for about a week.

5. Leave the picture to dry completely before putting it into your frame.

SUMMER – CHECK IT!

Have you done everything in summer to prepare your garden for the autumn months? Here is a checklist of the activities we've talked about this season. There is also a guide to help you choose some of the nicest summer plants for your garden.

Have you...

☐ Put up a bat box?

☐ Mowed the lawn?

☐ Dug out lawn weeds if there are too many?

☐ Planted pots with pelargoniums?

☐ Dead-headed your flowers?

☐ Sowed vegetable seeds and thinned them?

☐ Made a herb garden and dried some herbs?

☐ Watered and fed your plants?

☐ Grown some tomatoes?

☐ Made pot-pourri?

☐ Planted a rock garden?

☐ Checked fruit and vegetables for ripening?

☐ Collected seeds for sowing next year?

☐ Sowed seeds of autumn crops?

☐ Taken cuttings?

☐ Made a pressed flower picture?

Top plants that flower in summer

Clematis

Cosmos

Dahlia

Rose

Geranium

Sunflower

Red Hot Poker

Marigold

Larkspur

Autumn

Early Autumn

What's going on in the garden?

You will notice the weather is beginning to feel much cooler – and the days are getting shorter. It is dark earlier in the evening. This is a sure sign winter is coming, and plants and animals of all kinds must prepare for it. But all living things have their own ways of making life easy.

Trees stop growing and the leafy deciduous kinds shed their leaves. Perennial plants stay alive below ground where their roots are safe and protected but their shoots and leaves die.

Many insects and other small creatures hibernate – they simply go to sleep so they need no food. A few mammals – bats, hedgehogs and dormice – hibernate too.

Birds do not sleep through the winter. They either find enough food or they migrate to warmer countries.

We are approaching the time of the year when we can expect strong winds or gales. Plants are designed to withstand wind but it's useful to give some of them a little help. Young trees can be damaged – not because they are likely to be snapped, they are too bendy for that – but because they will rock backwards and forwards in the soil and this loosens their roots. Make sure any young trees have strong posts next to them and use a special plastic tree tie to fix them to it.

Fungi

Fungi aren't really plants and they aren't animals, but they are living things and they are all around us. Perhaps you will know them best as mushrooms or toadstools. Moulds are also kinds of fungi and can cause diseases that may affect our plants. But fungi can be very useful in the garden.

There are many tiny fungi living invisibly in the soil and in the compost bin. Some of these help to rot all the garden waste and turn it into plant food, and others help plants absorb food. They do this by forming a kind of mould that wraps around the plant's roots and soaks up food from the soil.

Fungi don't need seeds. Instead, they reproduce by spreading tiny spores which are much smaller than seeds and can only be seen with a microscope.

What's happening to the plants?

One of the big changes in early autumn is that annual flowers are fading and most of the colour over the next few months will come from perennial plants. Some of the loveliest flowers in the autumn are on climbing plants – or climbers, as they are usually called. They are important in the garden because they add height *(see below right)* – they make the garden seem taller – and they make people look upwards as well as downwards!

Some of the prettiest climbing plants for the autumn are varieties of Clematis *(see below left)*. One lovely kind is called *Orange Peel*. They are easy to grow and you will find them at most garden centres. They are best planted in a wilder part of the garden. They are too vigorous to grow against a house wall. In the spring, you should prune them back to about 60 centimetres above soil level. It sounds cruel but they will thrive afterwards.

Climbing plants usually grow in dry sheltered conditions close to walls or trees so they need extra compost in the planting hole and extra water while they are growing too.

Keep the garden tidy

After you've collected the vegctables, and as flowers come to the end of their lives, it's important not to leave them all in the ground. Some flowers may have seed heads and these can be left for birds to feed on. But once the birds have eaten everything, the old plants will look untidy and will also attract diseases that could spread to other plants. So dig or pull them up as soon as they are finished with, and take them to the compost bin (see page 81). Clear away crops as they are harvested.

What can I do in the garden?

Store fruit and vegetables

It is very satisfying to be able to save some of your crops for use during the winter. There are several ways you can do this. Some vegetables can stay where they are growing, and unless you live in an extremely cold area they will be all right outside.

Apples

You can store apples one beside another on shelves, in paper trays or in groups of ten or twelve in clean, dry plastic food bags – but make sure the bags have a few holes in them to let the air in. You should only store undamaged apples. None of them should show any signs of a broken skin or they will rot. Never store any apples that you have dropped! Only pick them from the tree and not from the ground.

Pears

These will not keep as long as apples and are better stored singly, but check them every few days as they ripen quickly. You don't want to miss them when they turn juicy and delicious.

Carrots, parsnips, beetroot

Leave these in the ground until you want to eat them.

Brussels sprouts and broccoli

These will grow right through the coldest months.

Dig potatoes

Your potatoes should be dug up now. Choose a sunny day so the ground will not be too wet. You must be very careful when you are digging, as it's very easy to stick your fork right through the potato tubers. It's a good idea to pick up even the tiny ones that are too small to eat because if they are left in the soil, they may grow next year – and you will then have potatoes among your new plants.

You will need

- a garden fork
- strong paper bags

1. Push your garden fork deeply into the soil at least 15 centimetres away from the plant, so you can lever up the potatoes from below.

2. As the potatoes come to the surface, collect them by hand. Gently brush off the soil and let them lie for a few hours on the surface of the ground to dry.

3. Collect them up and store them in strong paper bags. Don't use plastic bags as the potatoes will become wet and rot. Keep the bags in a cool place – and check them every so often to be sure that none are going rotten. Remove the damaged ones.

Make it! Spore print

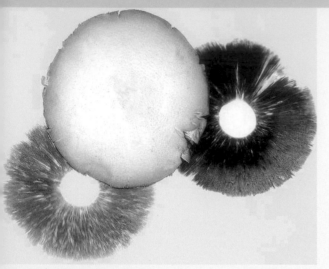

First collect a ripe toadstool from the garden or use a mushroom from the supermarket. It should be fully open – not one that is still closed like a 'button' mushroom. If you look at the underside of the mushroom, where the stalk is, you will see a mass of thin, wavy flaps called gills. The spores grow on the gills.

You will need

- a mushroom or toadstool
- scissors
- white paper
- a glass or jar

1. To make your spore print, cut the cap off the stalk and place it gills downward on to a sheet of white paper.

2. Place a glass or empty jar over the top to trap moisture inside and leave it for about twelve hours.

3. Then take off the jar and carefully lift the cap. You will find the pattern of the gills on the paper – this is caused by the spores dropping from them in the moist conditions. See how tiny the spores are. Each of these will grow into a new mushroom if it finds a good patch of damp earth.

Warning!
Most kinds of mushrooms and toadstools are safe to eat but a few types are very poisonous. Never eat a mushroom or toadstool unless an adult tells you it is safe. If you touch a toadstool in the wild, make sure you wash your hands afterwards.

Mid Autumn

What's going on in the garden?

This is one of the most colourful times of the year in the garden and the countryside – but not because of the flowers. It is because of the beautiful reds, yellows and oranges of the trees. Have you ever wondered why leaves change colour in this way – and why some trees do it more than others?

Only leafy or deciduous trees change colour. They shed their leaves in autumn and change colour just before they drop.

Their leaves change because the trees use them like a rubbish bin, and waste chemicals from inside the tree are transferred into the leaves before they fall. Some of these chemicals are coloured. But because the winter is coming and the tree will stop growing, it stops making green chlorophyll – which is the chemical needed to make plant food. Then these other, more brightly coloured leaf chemicals can be seen. Evergreen trees are different. They don't actually keep their leaves forever but they drop them in small numbers through the year so the trees always look the same.

What's happening to the plants?

Your fruits are continuing to ripen and the late season vegetables are ready for digging. The winter vegetables that we sowed in the spring will soon be ready.

Grass has almost stopped growing. When it is mown at this time of the year, there is not much to cut off. It's important not to mow the grass too closely now. If the grass is cut low, it will encourage moss and other weeds to grow.

What can I do in the garden?

Make your own compost

Did you know that much of the kitchen and garden waste we throw away could actually be recycled? Vegetable and plant matter can be rotted down to make compost, and it can be dug back into the soil where it will help plants to grow. It does this by making the soil into a lovely crumbly texture that is good for roots and it contains some plant food too.

Compost should be made in a compost bin and there are several kinds of these. You can buy them in your local garden centre. Some are shaped like big wooden boxes, others are plastic and shaped like barrels. Use any vegetable waste from the kitchen – but not meat or any other animal scraps. It's also not a good idea to add leaves to the compost bin as they rot much more slowly than other material and may block it.

Compost should be ready to dig into the garden soil in about six months – but be careful when you take it out of the bin. Hedgehogs and other animals, including grass snakes, hibernate in compost so be sure you don't harm them with your fork. It is best to add compost to the garden in autumn or early spring.

You will need:
- a compost bin
- compost accelerator
- leftover kitchen scraps
- garden waste

1. Add your leftover kitchen scraps and garden waste to your compost bin in layers about 20 centimetres deep.

3. There needs to be a little moisture in the bin so in dry spells you may need to dampen the compost bin contents with a watering can or a hosepipe.

2. Scatter compost accelerator over each layer as you put them in the bin. You will find compost accelerator at your garden centre. It provides food for the bacteria and fungi to start growing and rot the waste material.

4. In a very rainy spell, you might need to cover your bin with a plastic sheet to prevent it becoming too wet.

Plant daffodil, crocus and tulip bulbs

This is the best time to plant bulbs. Shops, garden centres and even supermarkets have a huge assortment for sale at this time of year. There are really three different kinds – bulbs, corms and tubers. They are fat and often lumpy because they are full of plant food. A bulb is a kind of bud, a corm is a swollen stem and a tuber is either a swollen stem or a swollen root. Because bulbs have so much food stored inside them, the plant can begin growing without having to find food in the soil. This means they can grow very quickly and often very early in the year – even before the soil has started to warm up. If you plant them now, they will be some of the first plants to flower in spring.

Some of the most popular bulbs used in gardens are daffodils, crocuses and tulips. There are many types to choose from. Crocuses are very reliable and none of them grow very tall.

Remember too that all bulbs look lovely in pots *(see left)*. Try planting large bulbs deeper and smaller ones nearer the surface. You will have double the effect!

If you choose hyacinth bulbs that are sold especially for growing indoors, you should have lovely fragrant flowers in time for Christmas.

**For planting in the garden
you will need:**

• daffodil, crocus and tulip bulbs

• a trowel or spade

• a small bag of sand

3. Place the bulbs on the sand with spaces in between them about equal to the size of the bulb.

1. Plant bulbs in groups as a bulb on its own looks a bit lonely and won't be as attractive. Use a spade or trowel to dig a hole about three times deeper than the size of the bulbs. For big bulbs you will need a hole about 15 centimetres deep.

4. Carefully put the soil back. Then wait for the exciting moment next spring when they start to emerge!

2. Scatter a little sand in the bottom – this will help to stop the bulbs rotting.

In pots, use a good potting compost and plant the bulbs to the same depth and spacing as in the garden. The number of bulbs you can fit in will depend on the size of the pot.

Make it! Halloween lantern

If you grew a pumpkin this year (see page 37) it will ready about now. Here is a great idea for using your pumpkin.

You will need:

- a sharp knife
- a spoon
- a bowl for the flesh
- a pen
- a candle or tea-light and a holder

1. Cut the top off a large pumpkin with a knife.

2. The inside is hollow, but scrape some of the pumpkin flesh away from the walls with a spoon. This can be quite hard work – so get someone to help you if you need to. Put the flesh in a bowl. You can use it to make pumpkin soup later.

85

3. Draw a face on the outside of the pumpkin with a pen.

4. Carefully cut out eyes and mouth with the sharp knife.

5. Place a candle or a tea-light in a small holder and carefully light it and place it inside the pumpkin – a spooky sight for Halloween! Remember that you should never leave a lit candle or tea-light.

Late Autumn

What's going on in the garden?

Birds should be welcome in everyone's garden. They are beautiful and interesting to watch and they are also helpful to gardeners because they eat weed seeds and many insect pests. It's true that sometimes they can cause harm – they may eat fruit and they peck holes in the lawn – but we can put netting over the fruit to protect it and the lawn won't be badly damaged. At this time of the year, food is becoming harder for birds to find so if you made a bird table in the spring, it is important to keep it well-stocked with food. If you don't have a bird table, hang a bird-feeder from a tree or from a hook outside your window.

The RSPB and the British Trust for Ornithology (ornithology is the name for the study of birds) welcomes young members. Why not visit a few bird reserves where you will see many species that don't visit our gardens?

What's happening to the plants?

We can expect frost at any time now. During the night, it can get so cold that water vapour in the air freezes and forms ice. In the morning, we can see the soft white covering on everything in the garden. It looks very beautiful but frost can be a problem for gardeners as it freezes tender plants. Once the ice melts, any tender plants still outside may turn black and floppy and should be cleared away.

Tender plants like pelargoniums, fuchsias and Marguerite daisies that you want to keep for next year should be dug up and put in pots before the frosts arrive. Keep them somewhere frost-free like a greenhouse or garage (provided it has windows and isn't too dark) but give them almost no water or they will rot.

There are now hardly any leaves left on the deciduous trees. The autumn winds have blown them off, but you should rake them from the garden as they make paths slippery and block drains. Gather them up and place them in a bin for recycling.

What can I do in the garden?

• Dig the soil

The soil is where we grow our plants, so we must look after it. Every year the plants take food from the soil and we need to replace this so we can grow new, strong plants year after year. We do this by adding compost and fertiliser.

All year round, we walk on the soil in our gardens and trample it down. We can't help this because we often need to reach the plants to look after them. When soil is walked on, the surface becomes smooth and hard. The rain can't drain into it and air doesn't reach inside so plants don't grow well. Digging the soil puts this right.

Only dig a small amount of soil at a time. It can be hard work and may make your arms and legs ache until you are used to it.

You will need:

- a garden fork
- a spade (for hard soil)
- a strong pair of boots
- compost

1. If the soil is really hard, you will need to use a spade. Push it into the ground with your foot and lift out the lump of soil.

2. Turn the lump of soil over and use the spade to break it up into small chunks. You don't need to smash it into tiny pieces – the weather will do that for you!

3. In areas where the soil is not packed too hard, you can use your fork to dig it and break it into finer pieces. You will need to do this again in the spring, and dig out any weeds before you plant or sow.

4. Add some compost from your compost bin. Use the fork to spread it on top of the soil and if you are feeling very strong, mix some of it into the soil. If you can't manage this, leave it on the surface and the gardener's best friends – the earthworms – will drag it down for you during the winter!

Plant a fruit tree

If you don't have any fruit trees or bushes in your garden, this is the best time
to plant them. There is a good range at most garden centres but you need to
take more care choosing fruit plants than normal trees and bushes. There are
many different varieties and they produce their fruit at different times. Some of
the most popular types to choose from are pear trees (*see above*) and apple trees.
With apples, decide whether you want an eating variety or a cooking variety.

Most apple trees won't produce fruit on their own. They need pollen
from another apple tree growing nearby – one that blossoms at the same
time. If you are lucky, there might be a suitable tree in your garden
already, or in a neighbour's garden. One simple solution is to choose
one of the family trees that we talked about on page 61 where there
are two varieties grafted on the same plant.

You will need:
- a spade
- a strong stake
- a tree tie

1. Dig a hole twice as big as the roots of your tree and deep enough for the whole root ball to fit inside.

2. Place the tree carefully in the hole and gently fill it with the soil. All the roots should be buried to protect the young tree from the cold weather to come.

3. Put a strong stake alongside to hold the tree upright. The stake should be about 2 centimetres from the trunk of the tree and about 1.5 metres high. Attach it with a special tree tie which you can buy at the garden centre. These are especially made so they won't cut into the bark and will expand as the tree grows bigger.

Tidy up

A tidy garden is a healthy garden. It's a garden where we don't leave plant pots and seed trays lying around and we pull up old plants as soon as they are finished. It's a garden where there aren't masses of weeds and tangles of bramble. In untidy gardens, pests and diseases will hide and breed and cause problems for our plants. However, it is good to keep one or two wild areas *(see below)* as these are important places for wild creatures. If you clear away all the old plant remains from the bottom of the hedges, many creatures – like hedgehogs – will have nowhere to live.

Make it! Bird seed garland

Why not make a sunflower garland that will provide extra food for the birds? You will need to remove the dead petals from your flower head before you begin.

You will need

- one of your large sunflower heads
- a sharp knife
- ribbon

1. Make a hole through the middle of one of your large sunflower heads.

2. Tie a ribbon around and tie it to a tree or to your bird table. It makes really welcome food for the birds and is pretty to look at. You could make several of these as birds really love sunflower seeds!

AUTUMN – CHECK IT!

Have you done everything in autumn to prepare your garden for the cold winter months? Here is a checklist of the activities we've talked about this season. There is also a guide to help you choose some lovely autumn-flowering plants for your garden.

Have you...

- ☐ Spotted a mushroom or toadstool?
- ☐ Planted a climber?
- ☐ Dug and stored your potatoes?
- ☐ Picked and stored your fruit?
- ☐ Kept your garden tidy?
- ☐ Made a fungus spore print?
- ☐ Built a compost bin?
- ☐ Planted bulbs for the spring?
- ☐ Made a Halloween lantern?
- ☐ Put food out for the birds?
- ☐ Dug the soil beds?
- ☐ Planted a fruit tree?
- ☐ Kept a wild area for animals and insects?
- ☐ Made a bird seed garland?

Top plants that flower in autumn

Clematis

Helenium

Michaelmas daisy

Nerine

Chrysanthemum

Toad lily

Rudbeckia

Japanese anemone

winter

Early Winter

What's going on in the garden?

Although the weather changes a lot throughout the year, the changes in winter are the most important for plants and animals. Very cold weather is a huge problem for the animals that live in our garden. How do they cope with winter? There are three possibilities – they either die, go to sleep or go somewhere warmer.

Many adult insects and other tiny creatures live for less than a year, so they die as the weather gets colder. They leave behind eggs or pupae which don't need to eat and which survive the cold to start growing in the spring.

A smaller number of creatures go to sleep for the winter. This is called hibernation and is different from normal sleep as it is very deep and the animals' whole bodies almost stop working. Some insects, amphibians and reptiles hibernate and so do a few mammals, such as bats, hedgehogs and dormice. These mammals hibernate because they feed on cold-blooded animals and they would have nothing to eat in winter. It is important to be very careful when we dig in the compost bin in winter because hedgehogs often sleep in there. If you find one, carefully cover it over again with compost and leaves and mark the spot so you don't disturb it again.

If you are very lucky, you might even find a hibernating grass snake too.

No birds hibernate in Britain but that's because they can fly so it's easier for them to take the third choice and go somewhere warmer. At the end of the summer, swallows and martins gather in large groups and get ready to fly south to Africa. You might see them perched on telephone wires before they set off. This is called migration. Some birds, such as robins, don't migrate and you can see them in your garden throughout the cold months. It is important to make sure you put food on your bird table to help them survive the winter.

What's happening to the plants?

Our gardens are looking bare and empty now. The leaves have fallen from the trees, there are few flowers because there are no insects to pollinate them, and non-woody plants have died down. But the beginning of the winter can be a lovely time. The air is starting to feel fresh and crisp – and in the mornings, the lawn is covered with dew.

When the garden and the countryside are looking bare, it's easy to find things that we didn't notice in the summer, and some of the most beautiful plants are just waiting for you to discover them. They are called mosses. None of them are very big so it's useful to have a magnifying glass to see them properly. You will find them on trees, on walls and rocks, at the side of streams and in other damp places, and on the ground under trees.

If you look closely, you may see tiny stalks with a swollen top – a bit like the shape of a lollipop. These contain spores. Like fungi, mosses have spores instead of seeds and flowers.

In some Japanese gardens, people make lawns of moss. They are very beautiful to look at but they aren't tough enough to walk on.

What can I do in the garden?

Check stored fruit and vegetables

You should check the fruits and vegetables that you carefully stored away in the autumn. A few may have turned mouldy and these should be thrown out so the rot doesn't spread to others. Any onions, potatoes or other plants that have produced stems or sprouts should be thrown out too. Add them to your compost bin (see page 81).

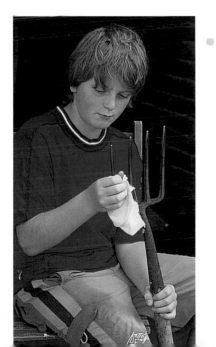

Pack away garden tools

It's time to put away the garden tools that we won't need again until the spring. Bamboo canes are valuable in giving support to our plants but if we leave soil on the bottom of them, it could be a hiding place for diseases.

You probably won't need the trowel and small hand fork for a few months so these too should be carefully cleaned. If there's room in the shed or garage, it's best to hang the tools on hooks.

101

You will need

- a bucket and hot soapy water
- bamboo canes
- garden tools
- lubrication oil

2. Carefully dry your metal tools with a piece of kitchen roll or an old towel to prevent them getting rusty.

1. Gently pull your bamboo canes from the soil and stand them in a bucket of hot soapy water. Stand your gardening tools in the bucket as well. Leave them for a few minutes until the soil is washed off.

3. When the tools are dry, add a little oil to the surfaces to give them some extra protection. If you look after your tools, they will last much longer.

Make it! Christmas garland

With Christmas coming, why not make a simple garland for your front door. If you like, you can personalise your garland using things from your own garden. Holly sprigs with berries, ivy and pine cones are excellent things to use. We like to use bendy twigs. Let your imagination run wild!

You will need:

- pine cones and long, bendy twigs
- gold or silver spray paint
- several sheets of newspaper
- wire frame (available from florist shops)
- curling ribbon and a bow to decorate

1. Collect some thin, bendy twigs – birch and beech are good. Collect three or four pine cones too. Spray them with silver or gold spray paint. Make sure you do this outside and put down newspaper to protect the ground.

2. Wind the twigs in bunches around a wire frame and tie them together with curling ribbon. Then thread through any sprigs from your garden, such as holly or ivy. Attach the sprayed cones and finish it off with a bow at the top.

Mid Winter

What's going on in the garden?

It's very exciting when we find creatures in our garden. Sometimes, however, we can tell they have visited us without our knowing – and winter is the best time to do this. If there is snow on the ground, you will see the tracks of animals and birds that have walked over it. With a little practice, you can even tell what kinds of animals they are because each has its own special footprint. Animals also leave tracks in mud and if the mud is smooth, you can make a real copy of them and start a collection. It's called making a plaster cast (see page 110). Unfortunately you can't make casts of tracks in snow because the snow will melt!

Change It!

Winter is also a good time to plan any
changes you want to make in the garden.
Perhaps you have seen things in other
gardens you have visited or perhaps you
like pictures of other gardens you've seen
in books and these have given you ideas.
Sometimes you will see a shrub or flower
you think would look good in your own
garden, and now is the time to decide
if it really would be suitable. Before you
try to persuade your parents to have
something new, use books or the internet
to find out more about the plant and the
conditions it likes.

There might be some changes in the garden that you think would improve
it without adding anything new. Perhaps there's a corner of the lawn that
is always difficult to mow or a plant that is growing somewhere too shady.
Perhaps part of your garden looks pretty but is too complicated to look after
or is difficult to reach (*see above right*). But don't move or dig up anything
without discussing it with your family first.

What's happening to the plants?

When there is not much colour in the garden, gardeners often say the structure is very important. The structure of a garden is its overall shape. Hedges, buildings, trees and walls are there all year round and if they are attractive, the garden too will become attractive, even without flowers. If you look at gardens in mid winter, you will see how evergreen trees and shrubs help the structure. Conifers are particularly important. Some of the common types of conifer that you will see in gardens are firs, pines *(see left)*, cypresses (most garden hedges are a kind of cypress) and spruces – the most common kind of Christmas tree is a species of spruce.

Conifers

Look carefully at a conifer and make a list of the ways it is different from a normal leafy tree like an oak or beech. Almost all conifers are evergreen, it is usually dark underneath them. Even one big conifer in a garden will create plenty of shade so imagine what it is like in a conifer forest. It is extremely dark because the sun hardly reaches down to ground level. This means that few other plants can grow and few animals live there.

At one time, most of the new forests that were planted in Britain to produce timber contained only conifers but people realised that this wasn't good for wildlife and so, as you travel the country, you will see mixtures of conifers and leafy trees in the newer forests.

Christmas Trees

It is not a good idea to replant your Christmas tree in the garden to use next year. They don't look right in most gardens, and they will become weaker every time they are dug up. It's better to have a Christmas tree that has been specially grown for use in one year – and is then shredded to make valuable compost.

The early weeks of the New Year are the quietest times in the garden, because it is usually the coldest time. But our winters are warmer than they used to be and it is possible to find flowers in sheltered places – even on New Year's Day. See if you can find early wild pansies *(see left)*, speedwells and primroses *(see right)*.

Plant names

Why are some plant names so long and why aren't they all in English? Most common garden plants do have English names – like Michaelmas daisy, onion and wallflower. But all plants also have another name. It's called the scientific name and we have to use this for those that don't have an English one. The scientific name is made up of two parts and they are usually in Latin – the language the Romans spoke. This is so that people in all countries will understand what we are talking about. If we said 'cauliflower' to someone from Russia or China, they probably wouldn't know what we meant! As you do more and more gardening, you will slowly begin to remember the scientific names and realise how useful they can be. The scientific name for the ornamental onion is *Allium hollandicum* (*see below left*) and for the courgette, *Cucurbita pepo* (*see below right*). It is not only plants that have a scientific name. Every living thing ever discovered has a scientific name. We have one too – the scientific name for human beings is *Homo sapiens*.

What can I do in the garden?

During the winter we don't have to take time to feed and water our plants and do tasks like weeding. This gives us a chance to attend to other things.

Look after the pond

If you have a pond in your garden with a fountain, it's a good idea to clean it with fresh water and a brush. This must be done by an adult but you can help. When the fountain is taken out of the water, you will see that it looks green and slimy. These are tiny green plants called algae and they should be removed so they don't clog up your fountain. When it has been cleaned out, it should be put back into the water. Never switch off your fountain in the winter, especially if you have fish in your pond. It adds oxygen to the water which the fish need to breathe. Moving water doesn't usually freeze and this means the fish down at the bottom of the pond won't die.

Sow early seeds

When it finally becomes too cold and wet to stay outside, there are some things we can do indoors. Although most seed sowing isn't done for several weeks, the very first seeds should be sown now, and you can do this indoors (see page 16). Sow seeds of plants that grow very slowly – like onions and snapdragons *(see right)* – in propagators in your house or in the greenhouse if you have one.

Make it! Cast an animal footprint

It is so exciting to see animal prints in the snow but if you want to make a cast of the print to keep, you will need to wait until a muddy day. Make sure you make your cast on a day when it is not expected to rain, and wear some old clothes so it doesn't matter if you spill any of the mixture.

You will need:

- plaster of Paris
- cardboard
- paperclips or sticky tape
- rubber gloves
- paint to decorate

1. Cut the cardboard into a strip about 5 centimetres wide. It must be long enough to be bent around the footprint you want to cast.

2. Bend the cardboard around the footprint to produce a hoop and secure the ends with a paperclip or a piece of sticky tape.

3. Mix the plaster of Paris with water until it is like a thick cream and carefully pour this into the hoop. You may want to use old rubber gloves to protect your hands.

5. You can either leave the cast white or you can paint it.

Don't forget to find out which animal made the tracks you have cast. The internet is often very useful or look in a wildlife book.

4. Leave it overnight to set hard then remove the cardboard and lift the plaster off the print.

111

Late Winter

What's going on in the garden?

On cold mornings, the garden can look especially beautiful with everything covered in frost or dew – and some of the most beautiful objects are cobwebs. It's only when you see them decorated in this way that you realise just how many spiders there must be in your garden. Many of them are sitting quietly and are fairly inactive at this time of year because they are cold-blooded. But spiders are among some of the most important animals in the garden. Some of them are extremely small and are called money spiders because they are supposed to bring luck and make you rich! A few kinds are rather large. Spiders are important to gardeners because they feed on other creatures and are extremely helpful in controlling garden pests.

If you look carefully at a spider, you will see it has eight legs. Spiders belong to a group of animals called arachnids and they are related to scorpions. There are some species of spider in the world that are poisonous but British spiders are harmless and are gardeners' friends.

Ladybirds

These are often found at this time of year hibernating in large numbers in holes in posts and similar places. They are a type of beetle and there are over 25 species in the UK. The commonest are red with different numbers of black spots. Both adult ladybirds and their larvae eat greenfly *(see right)* so they are especially valuable.

Beetles

Did you know there are more kinds of beetle than any other insect? Most of them are hibernating now but in warm places like the greenhouse – or even in a corner of your house – you might find some still active *(see left)*. Many kinds of beetle are good for the garden because they feed on pests but a few kinds, like weevils, can damage plants.

What's happening to the plants?

Spring is on the way because a few more flowers like snowdrops and some crocuses *(see left)* are appearing in the garden.

On warm days a few insects are starting to appear too but it's a dangerous time for them because if it turns cold again, they will die.

Catkins

You might wonder how early flowers stay alive if the weather stays cold. Without any insects, how are they pollinated? The answer is the wind. Some of the most important early flowers are called catkins *(see right)*. You will soon see lovely catkins on hazel bushes and they are like lamb's tails as they dangle from the twigs. The wind blows the pollen from one to another so pollination can take place. Usually, the flowers that are pollinated by the wind are not brightly coloured and not perfumed either. This is because they don't need to attract insects.

What can I do in the garden?

Grow vegetable tops indoors

Although some seeds have already been sown (see page 109), you must be patient for a few more weeks before you sow the rest. While you wait, why not try growing vegetable tops indoors. Collect the tops of carrots, parsnips or beetroot and set them up on a warm windowsill. Carrots are the easiest to grow this way.

You will need

- a sharp knife
- carrots, parsnips or beetroot
- a dish or tray
- coloured chippings (optional)

2. Arrange the tops in an attractive dish or a foil tray. You can brighten it up with coloured chippings in between the plants.

1. Cut off the top quarter from a root vegetable like a carrot, beetroot or parsnip – you may need help from an adult.

3. Pour in 1 centimetre of water and place the dish on a sunny windowsill but make sure it isn't too hot.

4. Look every day to check that the roots don't dry out. Top up the water if necessary.

5. Within a week your roots should have begun to sprout shoots.

Force rhubarb

Do you have any rhubarb in your garden? It is an interesting plant and late winter is a good time to try forcing some. Forcing is something that gardeners used to do with many vegetables in the days when there were no freezers or supermarkets and the only way to obtain fresh food was from the garden. Forcing makes them more tender and tasty – many of the old types of winter vegetables were tough and hard.

You will need:

• an old plant pot or a bucket with a hole in the bottom

1. Place your bucket or plant pot upside down over the rhubarb plant.

2. Because it is a bit warmer inside the pot or bucket, the plant will start to grow and it will grow upwards towards the hole, looking for the light.

3. The rhubarb stems will be thinner and softer and much more tasty! Why not use some of it to bake rhubarb crumble (see page 118)? Delicious!

Dig a new flower-bed

Outside in the garden you can continue to dig new flower borders but don't dig when the soil is very wet. Soil sticks to the spade – and to your boots – when it's wet so it would be too tiring. Wait for a few dry days before you start digging your new beds.

Prune fruit trees

This is a good time to prune fruit trees (see page 18), but this is one job that really should be done by an adult because it is very easy to cut off the wrong bits. Then you would have no fruit next year! If you carefully watch the pruning being done, you will be able to do it yourself next year.

Pruning young apple trees *(see below)* and pear trees is especially important if they are to produce plenty of fruit in the summer but very old fruit trees are best left alone as they will form a mass of small twigs if we prune them – and that means even more to do next year.

Plum trees should not be pruned now. They should be pruned in the late spring and early summer, because at other times the cut ends of the branches may become infected by spores of a very harmful fungus called silver leaf which can seriously harm the trees. But the fungus doesn't produce spores in the summer which is why it is safe to prune them then.

Make it! Rhubarb crumble

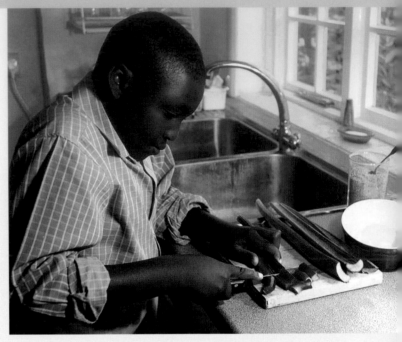

You will need

- 1kg (2½ lbs) of rhubarb
- 50g (¼ cup) of sugar

and for the crumble mixture

- 175g (1½ cups) of self-raising flour
- 100g (1 stick) of butter or margarine
- 100g (½ cup) of sugar

1. Choose slender stalks of fresh rhubarb, cut away the leafy parts and wash the stalks.

2. Cut the stalks into small pieces and put them in a greased baking dish.

3. Sprinkle the rhubarb with the sugar and leave for about half an hour.

6. Add the sugar for the crumble and rub it in again.

7. Sprinkle the mixture on top of the rhubarb and press it down gently.

8. Place the dish in the centre of a hot oven at 200°C (Gas Mark 6) and bake it for 30 minutes until it is golden brown. Always use special oven gloves so you don't burn yourself. Serve the crumble with custard or cream.

4. Put the flour in a large basin, then cut the butter into small cubes and add it to the flour.

5. Rub the mixture between your fingers until it feels like breadcrumbs.

WINTER – CHECK IT!

Have you done everything in winter to help your garden get ready for the spring? Here is a checklist of the activities we have talked about this season. We have also included a guide to what plants will be flowering in winter, to add colour to your garden through the coldest months.

Have you...

☐ Checked your stored fruit and vegetables?

☐ Cleaned and put away your garden tools?

☐ Made a Christmas garland?

☐ Planned any changes to your garden?

☐ Dug over the soil for next season?

☐ Collected up old and dead plants?

☐ Sowed seeds of slow-growing plants?

☐ Made animal footprint casts?

☐ Grown fun vegetable tops?

☐ Put forcing pots over the rhubarb?

☐ Pruned your fruit trees?

☐ Made a rhubarb crumble?

Top plants that flower in winter

Winter-flowering heather

Holly berries

Cornelian cherry

Witch hazel

Snowdrop

Winter-flowering jasmine

Primula

119

Glossary

Algae – simple green plants with no flowers, such as seaweed or green pond slime

Alpines – plants that grow naturally in mountain regions

Amphibians – animals such as frogs and toads that lay their eggs in water but also live on land

Annuals – plants that live their entire lives and produce seeds within one year

Arachnids – creatures with eight legs such as spiders and mites

Bacteria – microscopic living things that are found everywhere in our gardens, homes and even in our own bodies

British Trust for Ornithology – an organisation that makes scientific studies of birds.

Bud – the swollen part of a stem from which a new flower or leaf forms

Bulb – swollen buds that store food and help some plants to survive over winter, but often used generally to mean corms and tubers too

Chlorophyll – green colouring material in plants that enables them to make food using sunlight

Climate change – the gradual change in our weather patterns, sometimes called global warming although in fact some places are getting colder

Cold-blooded – animals that take on the temperature of their surroundings so their activity slows down in cold weather

Compost – this has two meanings: 1. rotting waste plant material that we use to return plant food to the soil *or* 2. a mixture of soil and other substances used to grow plants in containers

Compost bin – an open box used for making garden compost

Conifers – trees that produce cones instead of flowers, such as pines and firs

Corms – swollen base of a plant used to store food

Cuttings – pieces of a plant used to make more plants by persuading them to form roots

Dead-heading – cutting off old flower heads

Deciduous – a plant that sheds its leaves in autumn

Drill - a shallow groove made in the soil in which seeds are sown

Evergreen – a plant that sheds its leaves a few at a time through the year so we don't notice

Fertiliser – plant food

Fertilise – this has two meanings: 1. to feed the plant *or* 2. to pollinate flowers so they develop into seeds

Forcing– placing a bucket or pot over a plant to make the vegetables more tender to eat

Frost - occurs in cold weather in winter when water freezes and turns to ice and some plants may be damaged

Fruit – something formed on a plant to contain seeds, such as an apple or grape

Fungi – living things that look a bit like plants but have no green chlorophyll and don't form flowers, such as mushrooms, toadstools and mould

Germinate – to develop and grow from seeds or spores

Graft when parts of two plants are fused together and grow as one

Growing-bags – plastic bags of compost used like big plant pots for growing plants in places where there is no soil

Half-hardy – plants that come from warmer climates that grow in our gardens in summer but would not survive our cold winters

Hardy – not damaged by frost

Herbaceous – soft and leafy plants, not forming a woody stem

Hibernation – a deep sleep during the winter months

Insects – creatures with six legs

Larvae – young forms of many creatures that look different from the adults, such as caterpillars

Mammals – warm-blooded creatures with hair or fur, such as dogs, cats – and humans

Migration – the movement of animals (especially birds) from one region to another

Mosses – simple, small green plants that form spores instead of flowers and have very tiny leaves

Native species – animals and plants that live naturally in a particular region

Nectar – sugary liquid produced by flowers to attract insects

Perennials – plants that live for several years, such as lupins and Michaelmas daisies

Pods – types of long thin fruit that contain seeds, such as peas and beans

Pollen – a dust-like substance that sticks to the bodies of insects and is produced by male flowers to fertilise female flowers

Pollination – the action of pollen passing from male to female flowers

Propagator – small covered container in which seeds are sown

Prune – cut to shape

Pupae – a stage in the life of insects between larva and adult, sometimes called a chrysalis

Reptiles – cold-blooded animals that lay their eggs on land, such as lizards and snakes

Ripe – ready to drop from the plant or be eaten!

Root – the part of a plant below ground, used to provide anchorage and to absorb food and water

Royal Society for the Protection of Birds (also known as the RSPB) – an organisation that encourages people to care for and protect birds

Seedling – a young plant, newly emerged from a seed

Seed – something produced by a flowering plant from which a new plant grows after germination

Shrubs – woody plants that are smaller and bushier than trees

Side-shooting – pinching off the branches on tomato plants to leave a single upright stem

Soil – a mixture of rock fragments and organic matter in which plants grow and many creatures live

Sowing – placing seeds in the soil

Spores – tiny, dust-like particles that act like seeds for fungi, mosses and ferns

Stem – part of a plant on which leaves and flowers form

Succession – series of plants germinating from seeds one after the other

Tender – damaged by frost

Thinning – pulling out some plants to avoid overcrowding

Transplanted – dug up from one place to be planted again in another place

Tubers – swollen stems or roots used for food storage, such as potatoes

Warm-blooded animals able to keep their own body heat so they can stay active even when the outside temperature falls, such as birds and mammals

Weeding – removing weeds so garden plants can grow better

Weeds – wild plants that grow naturally in gardens

Woody – hard, like a tree trunk

PHOTOGRAPHIC ACKNOWLEDGEMENTS

a=above b=below l=left r=right c=centre

Jane Donald © FLL 19, 27, 30, 38

Andrew Lawson © FLL 88*ar*, 100*a*

Oxford Scientific (OSF) 111*c* (photo Mark Hamblin), 111*bl* (photo Les Stocker), 111*br* (photo Elliott Neep), 114*br* (photo Mark Hamblin)

Anthea Sieveking cover, back cover*l*, back cover*r*, jacket front flap, 5, 7, 10, 12–13, 14, 20, 22*ar*, 25, 26, 31, 32, 34*al*, 36, 40–41, 42, 45*ar*, 46, 48, 50, 52*ar*, 52*bl*, 53, 54, 55, 56*al*, 56*bc*, 58, 61*ar*, 68–69, 70, 74*a*, 75*cr*, 76, 77, 79, 80*br*, 83, 85, 86, 87, 88*bl*, 90, 96–97, 101*bl*, 103*ar*, 104, 110, 111*cr*, 112, 113*bl*, 118

INDEX